Major Scott

A Letter from Major Scott, to Philip Francis, Esq.

Second Edition

Major Scott

A Letter from Major Scott, to Philip Francis, Esq.
Second Edition

ISBN/EAN: 9783744763998

Printed in Europe, USA, Canada, Australia, Japan

Cover: Foto ©ninafisch / pixelio.de

More available books at **www.hansebooks.com**

LETTER

FROM

MAJOR SCOTT,

TO

PHILIP FRANCIS, Esq.

[Scott-Waring, John]

THE SECOND EDITION.

LONDON:

Printed for J. DEBRETT, opposite Burlington House, Piccadilly.

1791.

PREFACE.

IN publishing a second Edition of my Letter to Mr. Francis, I am happy in having an opportunity of saying, that the facts stated in the letter, have proved to the satisfaction of every candid man with whom I have conversed upon it, that the assertions made by the Chairman of the Court of Directors in the House, were strictly and literally true.

That a British governor should have added two millions three hundred thousand pounds a year to the revenue of the empire; that the King's Ministers and Parliament should have approved, and his successors should have followed his plans; that the people whom he governed for thirteen years should join almost as one man in bearing testimony to his merits; that agriculture, population, and commerce, should have been in a progressive state of improvement during his administration; that these facts should be proved by clear incontrovertible evidence, entered upon the Journals of Parliament, and most unequivocally acknowledged by the King's Ministers; but that the same British governor should remain four years impeached for the oppression, the ruin, and destruction in which he had involved the natives of Bengal, and for the loss and damage which the revenues sustained from his measures, are circumstances so wonderful in their nature, that an honest man will in future scarcely look for justice upon earth; for where shall it be sought, if it is not to to be found under a constitution which

boasts

boasts of such perfection, and in a jurisprudence of such purity, as are the constitution and jurisprudence of Great Britain.

Upon the Impeachment of Mr. Hastings much has been said and written by men of all descriptions. With the question of law I have never interfered; but under that of discretion I can say, that no gentleman can go into a mixed company in this great city, without hearing many a pious wish for the impeachment being brought to a close, yet it still " drags its slow length along," nor can any man form an idea as to the number of years which may be required to close the prosecution.

The American war was continued after the capture of two of our armies had destroyed all hopes of success.

The Impeachment of Mr. Hastings is continued after every man in the kingdom fees, that the great and material charges against him are totally false, and groundless.

I mean no offence by this expression, and I hope none will be taken, after I have explained myself.

Mr. Burke, that Proteus in politics, who first moved the impeachment, did it upon a ground that was very fair, and very intelligible.

Mr. Hastings was declared by Mr. Burke to be the scourge of the human race; that he had desolated provinces, broken the faith of treaties, violated private rights, reduced noble families to distress, and, in short, that he had brought every calamity upon a miserable people which can be comprehended under the expressive words in the articles, "oppression," "ruin," and "destruction."

These acts were the ground work of the impeachment; for, said Mr. Burke, "had he
"improved the public revenues and made
"a numerous people happy, I should not
"have inquired into the amount of his for-
"tune, nor should I too strictly have scru-
"tinized his actions."

Now this I affirm in the face of the whole world, and I say that Mr. Pitt and Mr. Dundas have again and again declared the fact to be, that the natives of Bengal were happier under the British administration than at any former period, and they as India Ministers have annually presented accounts, which prove the increase of the public revenue by the measures of Mr. Hastings; the ground, therefore, of Mr. Burke has slipped from under him, the great and material charges are totally false ; and without detracting from the consequence of that article (the contracts) which the present House has in its wisdom alone adopted, if put in competition with those which they have abandoned, it is a mere question, whether Mr. Hastings gave thirteen pence for a common necessary of life, which a more œconomical man might have purchased for a shilling.

The inconsistency in which the late parliament was involved, is indeed of a most singular nature.

By voting twenty articles of impeachment against Mr. Hastings, comprehending in them the strongest condemnation of *the system* by which India *was*, and *is*, held and governed, they fully and completely justified every statement that Mr. Fox ever gave, as a ground for his celebrated bill during its progress through the former House of Commons, and Mr. Fox might with great truth say, that he had fallen a sacrifice to low and pitiful intrigue, if the same Parliament which voted the twenty articles, had

had not also voted the resolutions moved four years successively by the India Minister Mr. Henry Dundas. These resolutions virtually justified *all* that Mr. Hastings had done, and proclaimed to the world that Bengal had *not* been plundered, oppressed, or destroyed, nor the revenues diminished, *during his administration.*

In short, with such contradictory matter before us, we ought in our closets to reject *articles, votes, and oratory*, and confine ourselves to the amount of the resources and expences in Bengal during Mr. Hastings's administration, to the declarations of the People of India, and to such unbiassed evidence as the Managers themselves have produced in Westminster Hall.

By this mass of indisputable, undisputed evidence, the following facts are established:

1ft, That Mr. Haftings increafed the refources of Bengal above two millions three hundred thoufand pounds during his adminiftration.

2dly, That the peace eftablifhment fixed for Bengal by Mr. Dundas was higher by above one million fterling than the peace eftablifhment of Mr. Haftings.

3dly, That the expences of the prefent *partial* war, greatly exceed thofe of the laft *general* war in India.

4thly, That the natives of India, of all ranks, fects, and religions, have concurred in expreffing their fenfe of the merits of Mr. Haftings.

5thly, That Bengal increafed during his adminiftration, and is ftill increafing in agriculture, population, and commerce, under that fyftem which he had formed, to which

His Majesty's Ministers annually enjoin the closest adherence, but at the same time, annually join the prosecutors of Mr. Hastings in arraigning it before the High Court of Justice in Westminster Hall.

It has been observed in some of the opposition papers, that I have paid many compliments to Mr. Francis, but that I have vented all my indignation (as they are pleased to term it) against Mr. Pitt, and Mr. Dundas.

I have certainly given Mr. Francis and his colleagues credit for consistency from the moment this Impeachment commenced. Yet I do not despair of their following (with some exceptions) the example of Mr. Bastard, who believing that Mr. Hastings had desolated provinces and diminished the public resources, voted for his Impeachment: but having received proofs that these charges were false, altered his opinion, and had the manlinefs rather to confefs an error than to perfift in it. Mr. Francis and his friends appear to me at the prefent moment to reject as untrue, the moft incontrovertible evidence, provided it clafhes with their favourite notions; I rejoice, therefore, that they are not the judges of Mr. Haftings, and I rejoice that their ftatements have not made the flighteft impreffion upon the minds of the public.

But having faid thus much of the gentleman in oppofition, I muft fay, that it is impoffible upon any principle of juftice to account for the conduct of Mr. Pitt and Mr. Dundas, to whom, as Minifters, a great and important truft has been delegated.

They know, and *they* have repeatedly declared, that Bengal was neither oppreffed, plundered, nor deftroyed by Mr. Haftings. They voted *once* againft the charge in toto, which contained thefe expreffions;
but

but being then left in a minority, they never again agitated the matter, but gave their vote and their influence for the charge when it was finally paſſed, though that charge has really, and truly falſified every ſtatement that they have given in ſucceſſive years, of the proſperous ſtate of Bengal.

Again in the Benares article, which turned in fact, upon a principle of taxation. Mr. Pitt in the ſtrongeſt manner juſtified the principle, but without coming again to any diviſion, or ever after agitating that queſtion, though he ſolemnly pledged himſelf to agitate it, he ſuffered Mr. Haſtings to be impeached for calling his principle into practice, in the hour of emergency.

And afterwards under the head of contracts—Mr. Pitt rejected the whole, except two, (the bullock and opium contracts) affirming that two others for which Mr. Burke contended, were not only free from blame, but

but highly meritorious, and that by one, he had in the moſt ſure and œconomical a manner, preſerved a nation from periſhing by famine.

Now ſuppoſing Mr. Pitt had moved the amendments as he propoſed, and ſuppoſing his opinions had had that weight with the Houſe, which for ſeven years they generally have had, what a ſkeleton of an Impeachment it would have been, when compared to what it is!! I conceive leſs than ten days would have been ſufficient for proſecution, defence, and judgment.

The nation would have ſaved at leaſt forty thouſand pounds, an individual would have been ſecured from an oppreſſion of the firſt magnitude, and the Miniſters would not have incurred the odium which ſooner or later muſt attend the man, who on one day pronounces thoſe acts to be criminal, to
which

which upon another he gives his warmeſt approbation.

I well know that Mr. Pitt could not command the late Parliament, and God forbid that ſuch a power ſhould at any time be in the hands of a Miniſter, but he could have performed his own ſolemn promiſe; he could have done what he did laſt year when he was left in a minority, in a bill for regulating the Slave Trade. He could have moved amendments upon the report, and if he had ſo done, I believe in my conſcience they would have been carried by a great majority.

The preceding obſervations apply to the firſt ſeven articles only. Of the remaining thirteen, having ſaid and written ſo much, it is merely for the purpoſe of bringing the ſubject completely before the public, I now repeat, that theſe articles were voted by the Houſe three days before they were printed,

of

of courſe they were not read; they affirm a ſyſtem to be highly criminal, which Mr. Henry Dundas, the India Miniſter, ordered *to be invariably adhered to*, to which in three ſeveral letters to Bengal, he ſigned his approbation, with his approbation alſo of the principle on which it was formed, after a full conſideration, as he ſays, in one of the letters, of all the minutes and proceedings that had a relation to the ſubject.

An Engliſhman who does not look up with reſpect to the Houſe of Commons, muſt be a bad ſubject; but an Engliſhman who ſuppoſes the Houſe of Commons not to be as liable to error as any other body of men in the kingdom, muſt ſhut his eyes to conviction. A debt of two hundred and fifty millions contracted in one century, and four fifths of it in half that period, taxes impoſed upon every article that can be called a luxury or a neceſſary of life, and an empire diſmembered, tell us but too plainly, that thoſe mea-

measures to which Parliament has given its warmest approbation, have turned out very unfortunate indeed for the country; and if we are now able to exert ourselves and to raise the astonishing sum of seventeen millions within one year, it is more owing to the vigour and genius of the people, than to the wisdom of Ministers, or of former Parliaments.

There was a time when Mr. Burke would have most cordially agreed in this sentiment. There was a time when he went *farther* than *I* mean to go, when he said * " the dis- " tempers of monarchy were the great sub- " jects of apprehension and redress *in the last* " *century* ; *in this, the distempers of Parlia-* " *ment.*"

But Mr. Burke has been so frightened by the French Revolution, or Mr. Pitt has so

* Page 56 of Mr. Burke's " Present Discontents."

completely converted him, that he now speaks highly of every part of a constitution,† whose " merits are confirmed by long experience " *and an increasing* public strength and na- " tional prosperity."

The cause of the protraction of the trial of Mr. Hastings is now perfectly understood. The late House put seven questions upon the first seven articles, and one upon the last thirteen. Yet in strict justice as these twenty articles contain above fourteen hundred criminal allegations, there should have been fourteen hundred separate questions. If therefore the late House had originally proceeded with regularity, it must have abandoned all that this House has given up, and nine tenths at least of what it still retains.

As the late Parliament, like all others, was composed of gentlemen of enlightened

† Page 85 of Mr. Burke's Reflections.

minds,

minds, and as Mr. Burke tells us, that the Managers are men remarkable for their good nature; an indifferent perfon muft be ftruck with aftonifhment, at a perfeverance, which fome may think borders upon malignity. For the conduct of Mr. Fox, and thofe with whom he is connected, one may account by fuppofing them to be actuated by thofe paffions to which human nature is fubject. The tempeft that raged fo furioufly againft Mr. Fox in 1784, was firft raifed by the friends of the Eaft India Company, and Mr. Haftings.

Mr. Fox early declared his hoftility, and he has been an open and avowed enemy. Had we then fallen, it had not been by an ignoble wound, from the poniard of an affaffin.

The ufe that was made of the name and character of Mr. Haftings at that period, is perfectly well known to every man who has

has bestowed a thought upon the politics of Great Britain. I would not presume to call to the recollection of any man the honourable mention which Lord Thurlow then made of Mr. Hastings, if the facts which have since been proved in Westminster Hall did not fully justify his Lordship, for every sentence that he uttered. I will not quote the sentiments of Mr. George Hardinge, delivered with great force at that time, because I read them in my place in the House, upon a former occasion. But the following passage from Mr. Rous's speech in the House of Lords, is so exceedingly forcible and so strictly true, that I cannot forbear to insert it in this place.

" The human character is not formed in
" retirement and from the study of books;
" it grows from the scene in which man is
" destined to act. For what the scene to
" which I allude, has produced, I may re-
" fer your Lordships to what the servants of
" the

" the East India Company have written on
" the subjects of war, of policy and of com-
" merce. I might refer to those great
" names which have arisen in their service,
" who while Great Britain claims the fore-
" most rank among nations, may dispute
" the palm with the bravest and ablest of
" her sons. I might refer to the great and
" much injured man, *who is the more im-*
" *mediate object of our present attention*, I
" mean Mr. Hastings: possessed of every
" talent which can adorn and raise the sta-
" tion which he fills, indefatigable industry,
" penetrating sagacity, fertility in resource,
" but above all, that personal and political
" magnanimity, which bears him undis-
" mayed through every difficulty, and has
" enabled him not only to extricate us with-
" out loss, from a ruinous and extensive war,
" which in every other quarter of the globe
" has diminished the territories of Great
" Britain, but to snatch the laurels from the
" brow of the enemy, and by the victories
" in

"in the East in a degree to redeem the "losses, which, under a different conduct, "this unhappy country sustained in the "West."

Such was the character then given of Mr. Hastings. Those who have since seen his firmness and magnanimity, while arraigned as a criminal for acts then pronounced to be meritorious, can best determine the truth of Mr. Rous's description.

I have declared in the most public manner, that during the critical period which preceded the removal of Mr. Fox, I never asked directly or indirectly for favour or protection for Mr. Hastings, and whatever promises of support were given, came voluntary, and unsolicited by me. But I must have been unsufferably stupid indeed, not to have taken the precaution of insisting upon justice for Mr. Hastings, had I supposed it to be within possibility, that in less than three

three years, from the date of Mr. Fox's removal, the Minifter who came into power, by oppofing what he then called and what I yet call fallacious ftatements, fhould by his vote juftify every thing that Mr. Fox had faid, while in his fpeeches he approved and in his 'practice he adhered to the fyftems formed by Mr. Haftings.

I know the abilities of Mr. Fox too well not to be aware of the length to which he could pufh this argument in his own favour, could he have fupported by evidence, the articles which the late Houfe voted. Did I in my confcience believe thofe articles to be true, I would beg the forgivenefs of my God, my Country, and my King, for the fmall fhare which I formerly had in exciting the people to oppofe their reprefentatives. Will any man of common fenfe believe that I would have declined on the morning that Mr. Fox opened his India fyftem, to meet Mr. Sheridan, then in the
zenith

zenith of power, and his friends supported by a decided majority in both Houses, had Mr. Hastings instructed me under any possible circumstances, to bargain for his resignation, or for his future safety?

But to Mr. Hastings the consequences have been most serious, as far as a trial protracted to a length hitherto unknown, and at an expence which to an individual must be ruin, since even to the nation the amount is of moment, can make them serious.

He was in the public service, filling the first and most important office in the gift of Great Britain, at the close of a very long and calamitous war, when the King's Ministers were pleased to present a scheme for the better government of India.

This scheme they declared to be absolutely necessary for the salvation of India, which
was

was then, as the authors of the scheme said, on the brink of ruin, owing to the gross neglect, mismanagement, and corruption of Mr. Hastings.

Another great party opposed with their utmost force this plan of Mr. Fox, and they could not do it without placing Mr. Hastings in the front of the battle. The present Lord Chancellor, with a decision which marks his conduct upon all occasions, declared it to be perfectly absurd, to argue the merits of a bill which was professedly grounded upon the supposed delinquencies of Mr. Hastings, without entering fully into his character and conduct, which he did accordingly. The change followed, and Mr. Pitt continued three months a Minister, with a majority of the House of Commons against him.

By this proceeding, of which Mr. Hastings could have no knowledge until it was concluded, he unfortunately excited the resentment of a very powerful party in this kingdom, against which he had nothing to oppose, save a reliance upon the honour, the honesty, and the gratitude of those who had acquired power, in a great measure, by the incessant activity of his friends.

Before the return of Mr. Hastings to England, Mr. Dundas, the original India oracle in the House of Commons, had so far read his recantation, as to avow his satisfaction that a motion which he had himself made for the removal of Mr. Hastings had been successfully resisted, adding, that by the resistance, *India had been saved.*

On the return of Mr. Hastings, Mr. Burke gave notice of his intentions to prosecute him, and accordingly in the next year he presented a body of charges, which stated every act that Mr. Hastings had done in thirteen years, to be criminal.

The

The charges were not couched in language more abusive, than Mr. Burke has often applied to Mr. Pitt, to Mr. Dundas, and to Mr. Haſtings.

The tranſactions of the firſt year were to reject the Rohilla war, and to vote that ſomething was impeachcable in the Benares charge, Mr. Pitt expreſſly confining himſelf to one ſingle point, namely, that an intended fine for an actual offence, was higher than it ought to have been.

The next year the cauſe was reſumed with the celebrated Begum charge, when there appeared a very material alteration in the conduct of Mr. Pitt. He no longer, as in the firſt year, talked of the eminent ſervices of Mr. Haſtings, " that by exertions " almoſt beyond belief, he had preſerved " an empire in a ſeaſon of the utmoſt dan- " ger;" but with a table covered over with proofs of the diſtreſſes of the Company, and with proofs that by the acquifition of a large fum in fpecie in 1782, thofe diftreffes alone could have been removed, and India preferved, he affirmed, that becaufe a feparate peace had been concluded with Madajee Sindia, no neceffity could have exifted. In the courfe of that year he fometimes voted for, and fometimes, againft the charges, in their firft ftage.

It being determined that in feven charges there was fomething impeachable, a Committee was appointed to put that fomething into a regular, legal form. This Committee confifted of gentlemen from one fide of the Houfe, who very naturally included every criminal allegation originally in the charges. Mr. Pitt was bound in honour, and upon his own profeffed principles and declarations, to move his amendments, and to exert his whole force in carrying thofe amendments. This was due in juftice to his own character, to his country, and to Mr. Haftings,
but

but he never did it, and the confequence was, as I obferved before, that Mr. Haftings was arraigned as a criminal, for acts of which Mr. Pitt had expreffed the warmeft approbation.

If it fhall be afked, why did Mr. Pitt thus change his mind? I muft anfwer, I cannot tell—but my belief is, that if Mr. Pitt had moved his amendments, it would fo have reduced the articles, that the prefent Managers would have told him, "you and "your friends may carry fuch articles as "thefe are to the Lords—we will not."

Of the progrefs of the trial I fhall not fay a word, but upon the eulogium paffed upon Mr. Pitt's conftitutional conduct by Mr. Burke a few evenings ago, I muft make a few obfervations.

If the inconfiftency of Mr. Burke were any longer worth a man's trouble to expofe,

God

God knows the field is ample enough. He profeſſes to treat Mr. Pitt with reſpect now, and to have abandoned all his former acrimony, becauſe Mr. Pitt has dulcified and neutralized him, by his late conduct in a conſtitutional queſtion, meaning the Impeachment of Mr. Haſtings.

I will take but one of a hundred accuſations which Mr. Burke has at times brought againſt Mr. Pitt. It is this; " that " having paſſed *a corrupt act*, he has carried it " ſo corruptly into effect, that the conſolidated " corruption of ages falls ſhort of it in enormity—that all the acts and monuments in " the heroic times of Roman iniquity, does " not equal the gigantic corruption of this " ſingle act." Mr. Burke has at times applied coarſer epithets to other people, which proves that he is not always maſter of courtly language—but in point of ſubſtance, of ſerious accuſation, I defy any one man to prefer a more weighty charge againſt another, than

than Mr. Burke has here preferred againſt Mr. Pitt. But he is dulcified, neutralized, and I believe converted, becauſe Mr. Pitt having in the laſt Parliament voted for twenty articles, thirteen of which he never read, and of the remaining ſeven, diſapproved all the moſt material parts, has been pleaſed in the preſent Parliament to vote that the Impeachment ſtill continues. Becauſe Mr. Pitt has not been pleaſed even in this Parliament to diſcriminate at all, or to ſay what parts of the articles accord with his ideas, and what parts do not. My underſtanding is ſo muddy, that I can perceive nothing either ſo conſtitutional, or ſo juſt in this conduct, as ought to induce an honeſt man to be dulcified and neutralized to Mr. Pitt, provided that honeſt man had formerly accuſed him of acts of the moſt atrocious iniquity.

TO
PHILIP FRANCIS, Esq.

Bromley, 6th March, 1791.

SIR,

THE moderate, the temperate language which you have lately used in speaking of Mr. Hastings, induces me to hope, that we shall approach nearer to each other in opinion hereafter, than we have done for some years. In this letter, I do assure you, I mean not to revive old animosities. It were needless now to inquire into the motives

tives that induced you to depart from that honourable line, which you took in your firſt Parliamentary Speech, when you declared, "that you bore no enmity to Mr. Haſtings, and were convinced that he bore none to you, both of you being of tempers too warm to retain reſentment; your conteſt was at an end, and the hoſtilities it produced expired with it; and that Mr. Haſtings, though in many points you had differed, was undoubtedly a man of uncommon abilities."

It were needleſs now to inquire how it happened that the two great parties of the late Houſe of Commons, differing as wide as light is from darkneſs, as to the real points of criminality in Mr. Haſtings's conduct, yet jumped to the ſame concluſion, and joined in the vote of impeachment. And whatever difference of opinion there may be between me and the gentlemen with whom you have acted, I muſt
do

do you all the justice to say, that your conduct has been marked by the strictest consistency, while the King's Ministers, have, beyond all doubt, impeached Mr. Hastings for those systems, to which they have given their fullest approbation.

It appears to me, that you entertain some doubt whether this assertion, which I have so often made, is really founded in truth; it is to remove every doubt from your mind, and to prove the justice of Mr. Lushington's remarks, that I take the liberty of troubling you with this letter.

The subject has attracted much of the attention of the public, and will, you may be assured, attract its attention still more; for I perfectly agree with you, that if the present war should be of any continuance, it can only be maintained by adding fresh burthens to the heavy ones which the people of England now labour under, and that it will be another American war, in point of expence.

I am sure I may safely affirm, that in no possible point of view can this war be attributed to Mr. Hastings; nor can it be attributed to him, that the finances of India were in so embarrassed a state when it commenced, as to cause serious alarms in the breast of every man of reflection both at home and abroad.

I agree perfectly with you also, that the Company is dead and gone; that is to say, the political power was placed by Parliament so fully in the hands of the Board of Controul, by the bill of 1784, that the Ministers alone are responsible for every measure adopted in India since that period.

You well remember how much we differed in opinion in that year as to our future prospects in Bengal; I ventured then to predict,

predict, that there would be an available surplus in Bengal, of one hundred and fifty lacks of rupees a year; most people thought me too sanguine, but I drew my conclusions from the materials then transmitted by Mr. Hastings, and the truth has been, that the available surplus was one fourth higher than I estimated it at, owing to two causes; that the revenues have been much more productive, and the expences a little below my estimate. But this advantage has been more than counterbalanced by the enormous expences of the Carnatic and Bombay; whether necessary or not, it is no part of my business to inquire now, possibly with a view to the present war they were not improper.

You must agree with me, that Bengal is in a most flourishing situation indeed, since after the astonishing drains of money which it sustained during the last war, it has been able to afford great assistance to the Carnatic

Carnatic and to China, and to send each year an investment of nearly a million to England.

The point then to consider is, to whom is this flourishing situation of the country to be attributed? The Chairman of the Court of Directors says, to Mr. Hastings—I say so too.

You appear to doubt the fact, and in reply to the appeal that was made to us both, I will answer by a candid statement of facts, which you, I am sure, will well understand, and which you, I think, cannot possibly contradict.

The assertion of the Chairman was, that Mr. Hastings had received the Government of Bengal, when all its resoures were little more than three millions sterling a year; that they were improving during his administration, and that when he resigned, they were

were more than five, being an increase of above two millions sterling a year; that the country flourished under Mr. Hastings, and that Lord Cornwallis pursued the same system.

Here, then, is an assertion of fact; it must be true, or it must be false; I affirm it to be strictly true, and shall proceed to prove it beyond all doubt, happy in addressing myself to a gentleman, who from local knowledge, and distinguished ability, can correct me if I am wrong.

I shall first begin by stating our connections with the foreign Princes, and States of Indostan.

Mr. Hastings, as you know, has the credit of breaking that formidable confederacy, which was formed in 1779 for the destruction of the British power in India.

Moodajee

Moedajee Boofla, who was compelled to take a part in it, he bought off for sixteen lacks of rupees, in April 1781, after thirty thoufand Marattas had been inactive for fome months on the borders of Bengal. A perfect cordiality has fubfifted between the two governments ever fince, and Lord Cornwallis has now a Refident at the Court of Berar.

The Nizam he alfo drew off from the alliance, and converted him into a fincere friend.

With Madajee Sindia he concluded a feparate peace in October 1781, who then undertook to mediate a general peace with the Marattas, which was concluded in May 1782, and ratified in January 1783.

And here allow me to digrefs a moment, in order to inform you, that the delay in ratifying that peace was folely to be be imputed to the refolutions moved by Mr. Dundas in April 1782; thefe arrived at Poona in September, and the Marattas, naturally concluding that the power of Mr. Haftings was at an end, declined to ratify the peace, nor was it done until a gentleman whom I fent exprefs to India, arrived with an account of Lord Rockingham's deceafe, and the fuccefsful fupport which Mr. Haftings received from the Eaft India Company. You and I have fince heard Mr. Dundas exprefs his fatisfaction at that refiftance to his own motion, and we have alfo heard him declare, that India was faved by that refiftance. Every ftep which Mr. Dundas took during the late war, was calculated to weaken the Government in India; he wifely, now that he is a refponfible minifter, ftrengthens it by every means in his power.

The moft perfect good underftanding has continued between us and every branch of the Maratta State, from the conclufion of the peace to this time. Mr. David Anderfon was the firft Refident with Madajee Sindia; Mr. James Anderfon the fecond; both the particular friends of Mr. Haftings.

The Refident appointed by Earl Cornwallis in 1788, was Major William Palmer, who ftill fills the fame office, though ftiled in the articles of impeachment, the fecret, confidential agent and bribe broker of Mr. Haftings.

The two treaties lately concluded with the Marattas and the Nizam, of which Parliament has fo highly approved, originate in Mr. Haftings. Both powers were eager to conclude the fame alliance in 1783, and Mr. Fox urged as a reafon for wifhing to recal Mr. Haftings, when his bill was before Parliament, that he had attempted to unite all India in a new war againft Tippoo, with whom we were, in fact, then

at

at war. Mr. Fox is therefore moſt conſiſtent in all his India Politics; but I ſhould be very glad to aſk you, who poſſeſs induſtry, ability, and judgement, in what particular, be it ever ſo ſlight, does Lord Cornwallis, or the Board of Controul, deviate from the ſyſtem of foreign alliances and connections that Mr. Haſtings eſtabliſhed? Moſt aſſuredly in none; Mr. Fox may think the Board of Controul, Lord Cornwallis, Mr. Haſtings, and Parliament, totally wrong; but this is certain, that the ſyſtem Mr. Haſtings fixed, miniſters have followed, and Parliament has approved. In my opinion we were better able to continue the war in 1784, than we were to commence it laſt year.

Having gone through this part, I come next to the Princes and Chiefs dependent upon, or in alliance with Bengal, and I ſhall trace them by the map. The firſt, and who touches the Cachemerian Hills, is Fyzoola Cawn. I will not go into the caufes of difpute between this Chief and the Nabob of Oude, during the refidencies of Mr. Briftow and Mr. Middleton; but in 1783, thefe difputes were totally put an end to, by an agreement entered into under the mediation, rather than the agency of Major William Palmer. That agreement has been moft religioufly obferved ever fince: the late Houfe difcovered, what Fyzoola Cawn never could, that Mr. Haftings had ufed this Chief extremely ill, for Fyzoola Cawn has correfponded with Mr. Haftings fince his return to England; and in the letter he wrote to Sir John Macpherfon, all he afks is, that he will treat him with the fame kindnefs Mr. Haftings did.

The next is Muzuffer Jung, the Nabob of Furruckabad, dependent alfo upon Oude. Various means were tried to ferve this Prince; he conceived Mr. Haftings to have acted

acted with the best intentions in the world towards him, in appointing Residents at his own desire, and in withdrawing them afterwards by his own desire. By the 4th Article of the Treaty of Chunar, all interference was withdrawn, and after the late House had voted that article of the treaty to be criminal, *Lord Cornwallis confirmed* it, and the Board of Controul *approved of what his Lordship had done.* Muzuffer Jung has very lately expressed his astonishment that any man should conceive his friend and protector Mr. Hastings had ever used him ill. But we live in an age of discovery most certainly!

Here then you find that the two Chiefs dependent upon Oude, remain precisely as they were fixed by Mr. Hastings.

Oude is a kingdom in which, as you well know, we obtained a sort of influence that was never before heard of. The act,

act, (though originating in the connection formed with Sujah Dowlah, by Mr. Haſtings) was yours, and the advantage moſt undoubtedly was obtained by a very flagrant breach of an exiſting treaty. The Company drew from Oude between 1775 and 1784, above nine millions ſterling.

In December 1783, Mr. Haſtings withdrew every ſpecies of interference from Oude—*a meaſure to which Mr. Dundas figned his approbation* in April 1785, *and voted to impeach Mr. Haſtings for it in May* 1787; an inconfiſtency which I dare ſay you will join with me in reprobating; though Mr. Burke, whoſe life, as he tells us, has been paſſed in compromiſes, may not.

In April 1784, Mr. Haſtings concluded his arrangement with the Nabob of Oude, and in September 1785, Mr. Dundas ordered, *that it ſhould be invariably adhered to*;

But

But in May 1787, *he impeached Mr. Haftings for that arrangement.* ✓

On Lord Cornwallis's arrival in Sept. 1786, the Nabob fent his Minifter Hyder Beg Khan, to ftrengthen and confirm the agreement that had been concluded with Mr. Haftings.

His Lordfhip conceived fome additional battalions were neceffary in Oude, and the Nabob confented to the meafure; but in all other points he adhered to the *principles* laid down by Mr. Haftings, and approved by the Company; what he had done, being, as he fays himfelf, with a view to ftrengthen thofe principles and to render them permanent.

Mr. Dundas, in reply to this information, tells Lord Cornwallis, that *after an attentive confideration*, he approves the arrangement,

ment, *and the principles on which it was formed.*

After this plain and unadorned statement of facts, you and the whole world must agree with me, that with respect to foreign alliances, and to Princes and Chiefs dependent upon the Government of Bengal, Lord Cornwallis has most rigidly adhered to the system established by Mr. Hastings, *and approved by Mr. Dundas.*

Under that system the annual subsidy of fifty lacks from Oude has been most regularly paid, and even ten lacks advanced by Hyder Beg Khan, when Lord Cornwallis was in want of money. You know that this whole system is violently condemned by the articles of impeachment; and Mr. Hastings is stated to be in the highest degree criminal for adopting it; but that does not alter the fact. Let the disgrace of such noto-

notorious inconfiftency fall where it ought, the fact muft be ftill the fame.

I fhall now confider the ftate of our own provinces—beginning with Benares.

Whether the expulfion of Cheyt Sing was morally right, is not a fubject which I fhall here enter upon, but I will prove to you that it has been attended with great pecuniary advantages to the Eaft India Company, that it has produced very beneficial effects to the country, and that Lord Cornwallis purfues the fyftem which Mr. Haftings eftablifhed.

This Zemindary was transferred to us by the Nabob of Oude in the year 1775, and the rent paid by Cheyt Sing until 1781, was 22¼ lacks of Rupees a year, with five in addition as a fubfidy from 1778, when the war in Europe commenced.

From 1781 until this time, we have received an increafed rent of feventeen lacks a year. The confufion which naturally attends a revolt occafioned fome defalcation in the two firft years rent, but even that was not very confiderable; and fince that period the balances have been very trifling, in fome years no balance of any kind, and in others an increafed rent.

The police of the city of Benares, as regulated by Mr. Haftings, has attracted the attention of all Indoftan. It has occafioned a very great refort of Hindoos from every part of the Decan to that holy city, and Benares has been increafing in fize and population from the day of Cheyt Sing's expulfion until this time. Yet Mr. Burke took upon him to affert, and for a time obtained credit for the affertion, that Mr. Haftings, by appointing a Mahometan, chief magiftrate in the firft Hindoo city in India, had fhocked the feelings of every man in the

coun-

country. You know that this declaration is totally false in fact: Ally Ibrahim Cawn, the chief magistrate, is universally esteemed one of the most virtuous Mahometans in India, and he has been patronized and employed by Earl Cornwallis, precisely in the same manner as he was by Mr. Hastings. It is a fact of general notoriety that the city of Benares was at no time in so flourishing a state as since we assumed a more direct controul in its government.

There were many predictions, as I well remember, as to the future fate of the province. It was very roundly asserted, that the increased rent could not be paid, but experience has proved that it can, nor do I find any apprehension expressed from any quarter, of a failure hereafter. The present Resident, Mr. Jonathan Duncan was, as you well know, bred up under Mr. Hastings, and employed particularly by him, in all revenue business. The powers with which

which Mr. Haſtings veſted the Reſidents of Benares, Lord Cornwallis has not diminiſhed, on the contrary, he has conſiderably enlarged them, and the Rajah is ſtill further reduced, than he was in the time of Mr. Haſtings; or in other words, as Mr. Haſtings made the preſent Rajah much more dependent upon Bengal than Cheyt Sing was, Lord Cornwallis acting *upon the ſame principles*, has made him now a mere Bengal Zemindar. Will you point out to me any one alteration in the ſyſtem eſtabliſhed by Mr. Haſtings for Benares? except that ſort of change, which, by Mr. Burke's doctrine, muſt be miſchievous and criminal, namely, increaſing the Britiſh power in the province, and trampling upon the Rajah's privileges. In every part of the province conſiderable improvements have been made, and a new city has lately been erected near Mirzapore.

The

The progressive improvement in the province, is undoubtedly owing to the expulsion of Cheyt Sing; but I am far from thinking that we have a right to dispossess men of the countries which belong to them, because we can govern them better, and therefore his expulsion must be justified upon other grounds. I think now as I always did, and as every man must think, who will allow his reason to operate, that if there is any crime in that Rajah's expulsion, it is not Mr. Hastings, nor Mr. Francis who is the criminal, but his Majesty's Ministers and the Court of Directors are deeply responsible; and if I may take the same liberty with the late parliament on this subject, as my acquaintance Mr. George Rous has upon another, (the Regency) I will say that it was in the highest degree disgraceful to the House, to carry an article to the bar of the Lords, containing within itself a great number of articles, I believe not less than thirty-nine,

nine, without having come to a specific vote upon each of those articles.

By what criterion am I to judge of the opinions entertained by the members of the late House? Mr. Fox, in a very clear and manly way, stated that we were bound by solemn engagements not to demand, under any circumstances, one rupee from Cheyt Sing beyond his annual rent; that it was criminal in the first instance to make the demand, and highly criminal to punish him, for delaying to obey an illegal order. This is perfectly clear to every man's comprehension, and could only be answered by a declaration, that Mr. Hastings had affirmed in the year in which he made the demand, that he had a right by treaty to make it, that the attention of the King's Minister and the Court of Directors, was particularly called to this subject, because though you did not positively deny the right, you had some doubts in your mind. By their silence for three

three years, Mr. Haſtings had every reaſon to believe they concurred with him in this opinion, "that we were bound by no en-
"gagement to abſtain from the right inhe-
"rent in every government, of calling upon
"their ſubjects for extraordinary aids in
"times of emergency."

But Mr. Pitt defended the act in the fulleſt manner, and aſſerted that Cheyt Sing was criminal for his diſobedience, yet not in ſo great a degree as to juſtify Mr. Haſtings for forming a determination in his own mind, to impoſe upon him a fine of forty or fifty lacks of rupees. Britiſh juſtice is a term much uſed in the world, but I will appeal to you, whether in the courſe of your reading you have met with a tranſaction ſimilar to this, in the annals of any nation upon earth. God forbid that even the devil ſhould be impeached to all eternity; yet his crime is defined; he is our common enemy, and never happy but when leading us

aſtray;

aftray; but Mr. Haftings has had an eternal impeachment, that is to fay, eternal as applied to the laft parliament, and for crimes which that Parliament did not condefcend to fpecify. Their fentiments I cannot poffibly collect from their votes, becaufe the vote was not more than this, that in the Benares charge divided into four parts, and again fubdivided into five thoufand more, there was a fomething for which Mr. Haftings ought to be impeached. That fomething, faid Mr. Fox, is every thing; it is for originally making a demand contrary to a treaty, for perfevering three years in that demand, and then for expelling the Prince, who did not very willingly obey it. No, faid Mr. Pitt, the fomething is nothing at all that you have ftated. Mr. Haftings had as much merit in making the demands he did, as Cheyt Sing had demerit in daring to difobey the orders he received; but there fhould be a proportion between crimes and punifhment, and though the man was highly criminal,

minal, yet it was a crime, a high crime in Mr. Haſtings to propoſe to levy ſo enormous a fine as forty or fifty lacks for his delinquency.

You well know that Mr. Pitt ſolemnly pledged himſelf to move an amendment upon this article, by which the real ſenſe of the Houſe muſt have been collected; for ſome reaſon beſt known to himſelf, he did not perform that pledge. Mr. Fox's ideas were very naturally adopted by thoſe who framed the article, and the conſequence was that the late Houſe voted it without either a debate or a diviſion, and Mr. Haſtings was brought upon his trial in the name of all the Commons of Great Britain, for calling upon Cheyt Sing to contribute his proportion to the expences of the late war, though you, one of his council, had aſſented to the meaſure, though it was communicated to the Miniſter and to the Court of Directors, and the propriety

priety of the act never queftioned, until Cheyt Sing's refiftance had occafioned his expulfion.

I have been the more full upon the Benares bufinefs, becaufe it was one in which you had a very material concern. When the firft demand was made in 1778, you affented to it, but expreffed fome doubts as to the right. Thefe doubts drew from Mr. Haftings a moft explicit declaration of his fentiments. They were tranfmitted home, but never cenfured either by the Minifter, or by the Company. To the demand in the fecond year (1779) you alfo affented, but when Cheyt Sing refufed to pay, you objected to troops being fent in order to compel him. If the demand was right, it was furely right to enforce obedience to it.

In the third year (1780) you affented to the demand, and on an unexpected delay in the payment, after a folemn promife, from

from Cheyt Sing, that there should be no delay, you assented to a motion for two battalions being ordered to Benares, to enforce the board's orders, and to a fine of one lack being levied upon Cheyt Sing for his disobedience.

When Sir Eyre Coote in Oct. 1780, proposed to call upon Cheyt Sing for cavalry, in a most critical and alarming moment, you assented to that demand also, and soon after you quitted India. For the subsequent measures Mr. Hastings is solely responsible; but up to this period, how you could have been one of a committee that framed these acts into criminal articles, how you could have voted for them, has, I do assure you, at all times struck me with much astonishment. I will hope, and believe that the business now appears to you in a very different light from what it did, and when reason takes her turn to reign, we may all lament our indiscretions.

Having finished with Benares, I now proceed to Bengal, Bahar, and our part of Orissa. The revenues of these opulent kingdoms arise from land, salt, and opium. The two last sources of revenue were, as you well know, created by Mr. Hastings himself. It has always been your opinion, that the monopoly of opium ought to be totally abolished, and such was once the opinion of Mr. Dundas, which upon better information he abandoned. The writer of the 9th Report of the Select Committee, who professes to be indebted to you for all his knowledge, very strongly condemns this monopoly. It was for many years in the hands of the Company's Civil Servants at Patna, as fair, and as public a perquisite of office, as any of the fees received at the Exchequer, or as any of those sinecure places, which Mr. Pitt settles for life upon his friends.

Mr.

Mr. Haſtings was the firſt perſon who conceived the idea of making the Eaſt India Company a participator in the profits of this monopoly, and in 1775, he took the whole for the public. I have read with much attention your ſentiments upon this monopoly, and I perfectly agree with you, that it is bad policy, if opium is to be procured by contract, to grant that contract upon too low terms to any contractor. Keeping this principle in view, the Board granted the contract for two years to Mr. Griffiths, at 190 rupees a cheſt. He being the loweſt bidder of fourteen perſons, native and European, who offered to furniſh opium by contract. It is a certain fact, that the Company's ſervants at Patna, who as merchants would buy a commodity on the beſt terms for themſelves, never purchaſed it at ſo low a price. In 1777 this contract was granted for three years to Mr. Mackenzie on preciſely the ſame terms that Mr. Griffith had held it, yourſelf and General Clavering

being

being parties to it; for it was granted *unanimoufly*, when unanimity was not ufual. In 1780 it was again granted by the Board *unanimoufly* to Mr. Mackenzie for one year longer, on the fame terms, yourfelf and Mr. Wheler being then a majority of the Board. In 1781 it was granted for four years to Mr. Stephen Sulivan on the fame terms; and though I have no right to queftion any part of your conduct, yet I do affure you, no circumftance ever ftruck me with more aftonifhment than your joining in the vote to impeach Mr. Haftings for a tranfaction in which, if there was any thing wrong in it, you yourfelf were *particeps criminis*; for a tranfaction in which the principle that you laid down, and laid down well in 1775, was rigidly adhered to. When Mr. Sulivan's contract expired in 1785, it was again publicly advertifed, Sir John Macpherfon, the Governor General, obferving, that the Directors had difapproved of Mr. Sulivan's contract, although granted precifely upon the

the fame terms with that of all his predeceſſors.

I deteſt a quibble, let it come from any quarter. There was a clauſe in Mr. Mackenzie's contract, empowering the Company to annul it, *if they ſhould diſapprove of the monopoly*—of the *monopoly* they did not diſapprove, and therefore that clauſe was omitted in all ſubſequent opium contracts. It is ſtated in the 9th Report, that this omiſſion was criminal, but the aſſertion is ridiculouſly falſe. The Directors on the 23d of December 1778, acquieſced (and they would have been madmen if they had not) in the continuance of this *monopoly*; but what they diſapproved of was, that it had not again been put up to auction, in order that better terms for the Company might, if poſſible, have been procured. This order arrived in December 1779, yet the Board *unanimouſly*, yourſelf a member, granted Mr. Mackenzie the contract *for one year*

year longer, in May 1780. If difobedience was criminal, it was at this moment; and therefore the *renewal* of Mr. Mackenzie's contract is completely *funk*, both in the 9th Report, and in the Articles of Impeachment.

Now let me afk you, what alteration is there in the *fyftem* eftablifhed by Mr. Haftings? Prior to *his adminiftration*, opium was a monopoly for the benefit of individuals; *he* made it a monopoly *for the advantage of the Eaft-India Company.* To the clofe of his adminiftration it was granted by contract on the terms fixed in 1775; fince his refignation it has again been put up to auction, and now produces a greater advantage to the Company: but the fyftem was formed by Mr. Haftings, and to him is the Company indebted *for this branch of public revenue.*

Salt

Salt is another very great and very improving article of revenue, for which the Company is indebted to Mr. Haftings, *and to him alone.* His plan, as you well know, was oppofed by Mr. Wheler, Mr. Barwell, and yourfelf, and when your acquiefcence was at laft granted, *the refponfibility refted with Mr. Haftings,* with this declaration from you, that the advantages to refult from it were *very uncertain,* and would be *very inconfiderable.* The condemnation of this fcheme in the 9th Report of the Select Committee, fhews the exceffive folly and abfurdity, into which even a man of genius will run, when writing of a country, and upon a fubject of which he can know nothing. The fyftem laid down by Mr. Haftings is ftill adhered to. The falt is manufactured on the Company's account. The revenue, which in his time was more than fix hundred thoufand pounds a year, now exceeds eight hundred thoufand; at the outfet of this plan, Mr. Haftings fixed the emoluments of the agents at 15 per cent. and they all moſt honorably made fortunes, from that allowance. Mr. Burke eagerly ſeized upon this circumſtance as proper matter for crimination; but Mr. Pitt in this inſtance was juſt, and he was generous. He expreſſed an earneſt wiſh that *he* might have the good fortune to ſtrike out ſo great an additional revenue, and he would with pleaſure give up 15 per cent. to thoſe employed in the collection of it. The ſyſtem continues to the preſent hour, and the per centage Mr. Haſtings himſelf had lowered before he quitted the government.

The next and the great article of revenue is that ariſing from land.

On your arrival in Bengal, Oct. 1774, the revenues were collected through the medium of Provincial Councils. The gentlemen with whom you were aſſociated formed a decided majority againſt Mr. Haſtings; you

you were fuppofed to enjoy the fulleft confidence of the Britifh Minifter, and Mr. Haftings was an unprotected, unconnected individual.

The government of fuch a kingdom as Bengal thus devolving upon three gentlemen who were utter ftrangers to the language, manners, and cuftoms of the people they governed, it is not furprifing that Mr. Haftings conceived the mode of collecting the revenues through the agency of Provincial Councils, to be the beft that could be adopted, and as fuch, he recommended it to the Company. You thought it by far the worft; but it fo happened, that in the violent difputes in England in 1776, the Whigs joined with the friends of Mr. Haftings; and Lord North and Mr. John Robinfon were beat in their ftronghold, the India Houfe. When Colonel Monfon, and afterwards General Clavering died, Lord North, from the avowed enemy,

became so far the supporter of Mr. Hastings, as to renew three several times, his commission as Governor General of Bengal, and parliament consented to each renewal without one dissenting voice. His Lordship's motives he has publicly declared; "he con-
"tinued Mr. Hastings, because it was in a
"season of war of great danger, difficulty,
"and distress, because Mr. Hastings was a
"man of firmness and ability, and because
"he possessed the confidence of the East
"India Company."

Thus confirmed in office, Mr. Hastings, after your departure, abolished the Provincial Councils and formed his own plan, a plan however which he never did carry into execution completely; and therefore it is, I assert, that the system which he did in fact establish, continues to the present moment; that some small alteration has taken place in the detail, I allow, *but none in the system.*

The

The plan of Mr. Haſtings was exactly ſimilar to that of Lord Clive in this moſt material part, that except where it was abſolutely neceſſary to be otherwiſe, the revenues ſhould be entirely collected by the natives. He therefore aboliſhed the Provincial Councils, appointed a Committee of Revenue in Calcutta, and propoſed hereafter to recal all the chiefs and collectors, but thoſe of the frontier ſtations.

But except in the abolition of the Provincial Councils and the appointment of the Committee of Revenue, the plan never was carried into execution; chiefs or collectors were appointed to almoſt every place at which they are now ſtationed. Of the general plan of Mr. Haſtings, or its ſubſequent modifications, the Directors neither diſapproved nor approved, unleſs as the latter was implied in their appointment of Mr. Halhed to a ſeat in the Committee, and in their acknowledgements of Mr. Haſtings's

meritorious exertions in providing supplies during the war. In the year 1786, nearly two years after the institution of the Board of Controul, this plan of 1781 was taken under consideration, and a letter supposed to have been written by Mr. Boughton Rouse, was sent to Bengal, granting certain powers to the Governor General and Council which hitherto had been withheld, and which authorized a ten years settlement. The same letter impowered the government to divide the provinces of Bengal, Bahar, and Orissa, into collectorships, and the number was in consequence increased from twenty-three to thirty. The Committee of Revenue remained, and was to be termed the Board of Revenue in future, with a member of the Council for their President. It has been a work of infinite labour and difficulty to collect materials for the ground work of the ten years settlement, which is not yet concluded. It has been productive of much difference of opinion amongst the members
of

of the Board, and even between Lord Cornwallis and Mr. Shore, as appears by documents which I conclude you have infpected as well as myfelf, for I believe there is a waggon load of them at this moment in one of the Committee rooms; but unlefs we are to be overfet by a quibble, I fhould really be glad to know any thing like a change that has taken place *in the fyftem* eftablifhed by Mr. Haftings. When Mr. Anderfon and Mr. Shore made their fettlements, they did it in every practicable inftance with Zemindars, and their fucceflors have done the fame.

Since my arrival in Bengal in 1767, there have been various changes in the mode of collecting the landed revenue. From 1767 to 1769, they were completely under the management of Mahomed Reza Cawn. Mr. Verelft in 1769 fent fupervifors into feveral diftricts. Two Boards of Revenue were appointed in 1770, the one at Moorfhedabad, the other at Patna. In 1772, the change was

was made by Mr. Haſtings, which totally reverſed all former ſyſtems. He deprived Mahomed Reza Cawn, (by orders from home) of all power, and made Calcutta the ſeat of government. From that moment the ancient city of Moorſhedabad has been nothing more than the reſidence of a Nabob and his family ſubſiſting upon penſions, and Calcutta has increaſed in ſize and opulence beyond any city in the world, in the ſame ſpace of time.

In 1773, the collectors were withdrawn and ſix Provincial Councils were appointed, a ſcheme profeſſedly temporary, but which became of long continuance from your arrival, and the unfortunate contentions that followed. In 1781, theſe Councils were recalled and a Committee of Revenue appointed, which is ſtill continued. But in point of fact, all theſe ſeveral changes were merely modifications of *the ſyſtem which Mr. Haſtings eſtabliſhed in* 1772, when he formed

formed the Council of Calcutta into a Council of Revenue, and removed all the Revenue offices from Moorshedabad to Calcutta, under the immediate controul and superintendance of the Council.

I think it hardly possible that you can have seen the accounts of the annual collections in the last twenty years, without being struck by the very remarkable equality in the several years collections. The account is before Parliament, and has indeed been repeatedly published; but it may be of some use in the present moment to bring it into one point of view in Current Rupees; all the revenue accounts are kept in Siccas, but as Mr. Dundas has presented the accounts annually in his Budgets in Current Rupees, I have reduced them to that exchange, but without attending to fractions.

Years.	Lacks of Current Rupees.	
1772-3	297	This year Collectors were appointed.
1773-4	294	
1774-5	295	
1775-6	296	
1776-7	291	These eight years the revenues were under the Provincial Councils.
1777-8	286	
1778-9	290	
1779-80	288	
1780-1	282	
1781-2	301	
1782-3	299	
1783-4	300	These six years the revenues were collected under Mr. Hastings's new system.
1784-5	303	
1785-6	299	
1786-7	311	
1787-8	298	These three years they were collected under the alteration in detail ordered by the Board of Controul.
1788-9	315	
1789-90	308	

Admitting that Parliament has not been deceived by false accounts, I think it not possible for any gentleman to look into these particulars, without remarking that there could have been nothing oppressive in the

the plans adopted by Mr. Haſtings, ſince they have been attended by an increaſe in the land revenue, notwithſtanding the vaſt drains to which Bengal has been ſubject for ſo many years.

An attempt was certainly made, though very unſucceſsfully, to overturn a part of this account, by ſhewing that the *nett* receipts into the Company's treaſury, from the land revenues, were not ſo high ſince the abolition of the Provincial Councils as before; but Sir John Macpherſon had already replied to this aſſertion, by ſhewing that the additional expences incurred, were in fact the increaſed charges of Government; they were firſt reduced conſiderably in Bengal, and ſtill further reduced by orders from England.

It was the policy of Lord Clive to keep every Engliſhman as much as he could from the interior of the government, and to tranfact bufinefs of every kind, through the agency of Mahomed Reza Cawn. This was his laft and parting advice to Mr. Verelft, and it was faithfully followed until we began to be involved in very ferious difficulties. The Directors themfelves had the boldnefs to break the charm; they ordered Mr. Haftings, on his acceffion to the Government, to form a new plan for collecting the revenues, and to bring Mahomed Reza Cawn to a trial for his fuppofed delinquences. Then it was, (in 1772) that the fyftem was formed, and the revenue bufinefs grew familiar to the Company's fervants.

But the utmoft difference between the collections in any two years in this long period of eighteen years, is only two hundred and thirty thoufand pounds; in general the difference is very inconfiderable, and although there has been a confiderable increafe

in

in the land revenues, since the abolition of the Provincial Councils, it accounts for a very small part indeed of the increase of the *revenues* of the Bengal Government, *during Mr. Hastings's administration.*

The total resources the year preceding his administration, were three crores and thirteen lacks; they were the three last years of his administration, five crores and twenty-five lacks upon the average, being an increase of above two millions three hundred thousand pounds, and they are still annually increasing.

The increase proceeds from four sources, for all of which the Company *is solely indebted to Mr. Hastings.* Viz. Opium—Salt—Benares, and Oude.

During the governments of Lord Clive, Mr. Verelst, and Mr. Cartier, opium did

not

not produce a single rupee to the Company; Mr. Hastings first made it an article of revenue. It produced in his administration, five hundred and fourteen thousand and nine pounds sterling, and may now be fairly calculated, one year with another, at one hundred and twenty thousand pounds.

You know what infinite pains have been taken to impose upon the common sense of mankind, and to detract from the merit due to Mr. Hastings, *and to him alone*, for creating this branch of the public revenue. It is industriously concealed from the public that Mr. Sulivan had the contract for the same period, and upon precisely the same terms that Mr. Mackenzie had held it. We are not told, as the truth is, that Mr. Mackenzie got it on the same terms also, as his predecessor, to whom it was given; because he offered the lowest terms, of fourteen persons, who proposed to contract for it; but it it is reprefented as a moft corrupt and abominable tranfaction, becaufe Mr. Sulivan chofe in a few months to fell his contract to a gentleman rather than to run any rifk, and becaufe the gentleman to whom he fold it difpofed of it to another. But the original tranfaction is not by any manner changed by the act of Mr. Sulivan. The merit and the crime, if there be any, ftands thus: To Mr. Haftings, and to him exclufively, is the merit due, of having created this branch of revenue.

To Mr. Haftings, General Clavering, Colonel Monfon, Mr. Barwell, and yourfelf, the merit is due of having made this revenue as productive as poffible in 1775, by then giving the opium contract to the loweft bidder. To Mr. Haftings, General Clavering, Mr. Barwell, and yourfelf, is the demerit due, (if there be demerit in it) if not again advertifing for propofals in 1777,
when

when you granted the contract to Mr. Mackenzie for three years.

To Mr. Haſtings, Mr. Wheler, and yourſelf, is the demerit due, of having renewed this contract with Mr. Mackenzie for one year, in May 1780, although there was then before you an obſervation from the Directors that you ought in 1777, to have advertiſed for propoſals, and to have granted the contract to the loweſt bidder. Here then is the real point of criminality, and were Mr. Burke to ſpeak four days upon it, out of the ſeven *that he has contracted for*, he can make nothing more of it than I have ſtated. If the tranſaction be a job, I ſhould be very glad to compare it with ſome of thoſe jobs, for which the people of England are daily paying, though without receiving the ſmalleſt benefit in return. Were Mr. Pitt's eſcrutore to be rummaged as Mr. Haſtings's has been, for you have all his ſecrets, I fancy the public would find that

that much had been granted, and nothing by which *they* could benefit, received in return.

Salt, since our acquisition of Bengal, has produced as follows: ✓

Years.	£. Sterling.
1765-6	— —
1766-7	118,926
1767-8	144,218
1768-9	— —
1769-70	16,907
1770-1	70,914
1771-2	61,663
1772-3	45,027
1773-4	229,192
1774-5	130,263
1775-6 loss of	1,473
1776-7	139,012
1777-8	54,160
1778-9	63,697
1779-80	32,237
1780-1	8,427
1781-2	

Years.	£. Sterling.	
1781-2	321,912	
1782-3	605,646	
1783-4	603,076	
	Current Rupees.	
1784-5	62,52,948	Mr. Haſtings's plan.
1785-6	48,39,000	
1786-7	45,50,000	
1787-8	51,00,000	
1788-9	82,35,000	
1789-90	86,41,000	

The next additional ſource of revenue is from Benares, and it has produced as folows:

	Years.	Current Rupees.
In	1775-6	7,97,578
	1776-7	31,99,303
	1777-8	26,32,705
	1778-9	31,66,935
	1779-80	35,44,925
	1780-1	31,18,390
	1781-2	22,31,426

1782-3

Years.	Current Rupees.
1782-3	37,75,081
1783-4	43,69,025
1784-5	44,64,535
1785-6	37,47,627
1786-7	43,12,650
1787-8	43,67,524
1788-9	42,65,738
1789-90	46,84,450

Of the continuance of this revenue there cannot be a doubt; on the contrary, a confiderable increafe may be expected from falt petre and opium hereafter.

The refources drawn from Oude are as follows:

	Years.	Current Rupees.
In	1774-5-6	1,35,05,186
	1776-7	30,13,683
	1777-8	1,04,36,966
	1778-9	85,54,290
	1779-80	67,74,206
	1780-1	

Years.	Current Rupees.
1780-1	75,77,948
1781-2	1,37,96,228
1782-3	80,66,867
1783-4	83,89,357
1784-5	84,14,000
1785-6	37,50,000
1786-7	40,02,000
1787-8	52,03,603
1788-9	52,53,145
1789-90	53,39,073

You will scarcely deny Mr. Hastings the merit of striking out these additional sources of revenue, since he has been impeached for them all, the salt excepted, and that was made criminal by Mr. Burke, though to accommodate Mr. Pitt he withdrew the charge.

As my calculations are taken from the documents before Parliament, some branches of the resources are calculated in English money, and others in current rupees.

In justification of my friend Mr. Lushington, I will bring the whole into one point of view.

The opium, salt, increase of land revenue, Oude and Benares, produced during the administration of Mr. Hastings, additional funds to the amount of above fourteen millions sterling.

This is one way of proving the success of Mr. Hastings's measures; and if you try it another way, you will find that the total resources of his government the year he quitted it, were two millions three hundred thousand pounds more than they were the year preceding his accession to it; and what must carry conviction to the mind of a rational man that there is no deception, is this circumstance, that these resources have been

been increased to the amount of nearly three hundred thousand pounds since Mr. Hastings's resignation, owing principally to the additional quantity of salt manufactured; an irrefragable proof of the increasing population and prosperity of the country.

You undertook the arduous task of proving, that the measures of Mr. Hastings had been attended "with great loss and da-
" mage to the East-India Company, and
" with vexation, oppression, and destruc-
" tion, to the natives of Bengal."

Mr. Pitt defended Mr. Hastings. He most positively and solemnly denied, that the revenues had declined under his administration, and he affirmed that they were then in a most promising state; but Mr. Pitt, Mr. Dundas, Mr. Grenville, and Lord Mulgrave, the four members of the Board of Controul, were left in a minority. You had the honour of beating the Minister by
a ma-

a majority of fixteen in a Committee of the whole Houfe, and they then abandoned the revenues to your difcretion. To you I impute no blame for maintaining your opinion, if it is fincerely your opinion, though I wonder how a man of common fenfe can retain it, in oppofition to the moft pofitive evidence—but the India Minifter is deeply refponfible indeed, for not oppofing in every poffible ftage, an article of Impeachment which moft pointedly falfifies every reprefentation that he has ever given of the paft and prefent ftate of India.

In this article you took the lead, in others you merely gave your affiftance, but in this I imagine you will agree with me, that the articles are in all their moft material parts, a direct attack upon the fyftem by which India is now governed, and that Mr. Haftings has been brought to the bar of a Court of Juftice to anfwer for thofe exertions by which he faved India, and for the adoption of meafures

sures which have received the fullest approbation of his Majesty's Ministers, and of Parliament.

All parties in the House have concurred in speaking highly of Earl Cornwallis. To speak more in his praise than he merits, I hold to be impossible; but how it is possible to approve *generally* of Earl Cornwallis's measures, and to condemn *in the lump* those of Mr. Hastings, is to me the greatest of all absurdities.

That the systems, both foreign and domestic, which Mr. Hastings formed, Earl Cornwallis has continued, I have proved beyond the possibility of contradiction. His favourable opinion of Mr. Hastings is perfectly well known to many very respectable men in England. His Lordship must have read the proceedings in the trial of Mr. Hastings, and the Articles of Impeachment; he must know that Mr. Burke has publicly declared,

declared, "that Mr. Haſtings was hated and "deteſted throughout Indoſtan, and that "Bengal felt herſelf relieved from a weight, "under which ſhe had long groaned, when "he reſigned the government." The ſame ſentiments, though in other words, are to be found in the Articles. Lord Cornwallis has himſelf been the channel of conveyance for the moſt complete refutation that could poſſibly be given to theſe general aſſertions. His Lordſhip in Council tranſmitted to the Court of Directors, teſtimonials from natives of all ranks, and religions, in favour of Mr. Haſtings. Were theſe fraudulently obtained? The character of Earl Cornwallis is of itſelf a full anſwer to ſuch a queſtion. Would he participate in ſo foul an impoſition? Mr. Shore and Mr. Anderſon, and many other gentlemen, have told you in Weſtminſter Hall, that the natives thought very highly of Mr. Haſtings, and their own atteſtations in his favour, put the fact beyond all doubt.

The Impeachment of Mr. Haftings has brought about unions more wonderful than that of the lion and the lamb, of Prince Cantemir. Could you have fuppofed a few years ago that your friend, Mr. Burke, would have thought himfelf *perfectly fecure* when feated between perfons, " whofe gi-
" gantic corruption was not to be equalled
" by all the acts and monuments in the
" records of peculation, the confolidated
" corruption of ages, or amongft the pat-
" terns of exemplary plunder in the heroic
" times of Roman iniquity?" How muft the *imputed* fins of Mr. Haftings fink, in comparifon with the *actual crimes of Mr. Pitt and Mr. Dundas*, if Mr. Burke has not grofsly libelled them; yet have we lately heard him fpeak even *kindly* of thefe minifters. Does your friend mean to confefs that he accufed them of corruption in 1785 without a caufe? or does he argue thus?—
" My life has been a *life of compromifes*; I
" think of minifters as defpicably as I always did,

" did, but I am in want of their affiftance
" now, and I muft compromife in order to
" procure it."

However you may appear to the world, yet you muft have fome moments of ferious reflection as well as other men; and I defy you to reconcile any part of Mr. Burke's conduct, in the courfe of this Impeachment, to juftice, or to common fenfe. There only wanted his union with two men whom he he has defcribed as the laft, and moft defpicable of the human race, to wind up his political character. Is it poffible for man to commit a more enormous crime than Mr. Burke has charged upon Mr. Pitt and Mr. Dundas? To rob a Prince in alliance with the Britifh nation, whofe country was defolated by war, under the pretence of making him pay debts that he never contracted, and to do this for no public good, but in order to repay a rapacious, and corrupt body of men, for the expences they incurred in procuring feats in Parliament, is a crime of so atrocious a nature, that were every thing true, of which he has accused Mr. Haſtings, he muſt be a virtuous man, when compared with Mr. Pitt and Mr. Dundas.

Allow me before I conclude to ſhew you how difficult it is to diſtinguiſh right from wrong in politics, and to prove that acts which are highly criminal in Mr. Haſtings, are laudable in the greateſt poſſible degree in others.

Lord Macartney, when he took charge of the Government of Madras, repreſented, in a letter to Mr. Haſtings, the diſtreſſes of Fort St. George; and amongſt other ſubjects mentioned the arrears then due from the Rajah of Tanjore. Mr. Haſtings, in reply to this letter, makes the following obſervation:

On the Ganges, 26th July, 1780.

" The late President and Select Commit-
" tee informed us that the Rajah had re-
" fused to contribute a store of grain for the
" subsistence of the army, for which the
" President had written a letter to him, ex-
" pressive of his displeasure. This is a lan-
" guage so remote from my conception of
" the actual and absolute rights of your go-
" vernment, while it is charged with the
" entire defence of the State of which the
" Rajah is a member, and of his depen-
" dance, that I can scarce offer an opinion
" which shall not appear extravagant in the
" comparison. In a word, I think it im-
" proper, *at such a time,* to leave the Rajah
" an option to withhold a grain of his store,
" or a rupee of his treasury, *from the service*
" *of the general State,* and most heartily
" advise, that while that service, *in the*
" *present desperate condition of it, lasts,* the
" *whole* (with the single reservation of his
" own personal subsistence) *be taken out of*
" *his*

" *his hands*, in better truſt for the *public uſe*.
" Theſe are my public, not private ſenti-
" ments, and your Lordſhip is welcome to
" avail yourſelf of them, in any manner
" you pleaſe. Moſt heartily do I wiſh,
" they may be conformable to your own."

On the 28th of Auguſt, 1782, in the moſt critical moment of the war, when it was known that France was making her great effort to ruin us in India, the Court of Directors, Sir Henry Fletcher being the Chairman, ſent the following *reprimand* to Mr. Haſtings. Mr. Burke had previouſly mentioned the matter in Parliament.

" The ſentiments contained in the pre-
" ceding extract, are ſo diametrically op-
" poſite to thoſe which *we entertain* re-
" ſpecting *the rights of the Rajah of Tanjore*,
" and the other Powers connected with the
" Company, *and are ſo repugnant to every*
" *idea of juſtice and moderation, and the*
" *agree-*

" *agreements subsisting between us and the
" Rajah*, that we cannot but express our
" extreme surprize thereat. We hope and
" trust, that they have made no impression
" upon the minds of the Governor and
" Council of Fort St. George, *that may
" prove derogatory to the rights of the Rajah.*
" We have written a letter to his Excel-
" lency by this dispatch, a copy whereof
" is inclosed for your notice, wherein we
" have assured him *of our unalterable deter-
" mination to support and protect him in the
" management of his own territories*, accor-
" ding to the agreements subsisting between
" the Nabob of Arcot, the Rajah, and the
" Company, *and to guarantee to him and his
" family, the quiet possession of his country.*
" We have, therefore, given directions to
" our servants at Madras to govern them-
" selves, *in all their transactions* with the
" Rajah, *agreeable to these determinations.*"

Such

Such was the return which Mr. Haftings's zeal in the public fervice *then* met with— *precifely the fame circumftance has lately occurred.*

The Rajah of Tanjore has *again* fallen in arrear; and although a very recent treaty, concluded by Sir Archibald Campbell, prefcribes in exprefs terms the meafures which *fhall be taken*, when the Rajah *fhall fall in arrear* in his payments, the Government of Madras, not thinking that mode *efficient* for realizing the refources of the country, *fets afide the treaty without fcruple*, and takes the whole country into their own hands, thereby adopting, in its fulleft extent, the doctrine laid down by Mr. Haftings in the laft war, and fo ftrongly reprobated by the Court of Directors.

This is one extraordinary contradiction; allow me to bring *a few more* to your view.

Mr.

Mr. Hastings is impeached *for the loss and damage which he has brought upon the East India Company.*

He increased their resources *above two millions three hundred thousand pounds a year,* during his administration.

He is impeached for having *vexed, oppressed,* and *destroyed* the *natives* of *Bengal.*

The people of all ranks and religions declare the assertion *to be false*; and it is proved by undoubted evidence, by gentlemen of whose honour and integrity both of us are fully convinced, that the natives are happier under our administration than ever they were before; and that under the mild influence of the British Government, agriculture, population, and commerce, have very considerably increased.

He is impeached for *a wanton waste of the public money for private purposes.*

Mr. Dundas's peace establishment in Bengal was higher, *by above one million Sterling,* than the peace establishment of 1777-8, when Mr. Hastings and yourself were at Bengal.

The expences *of the present war,* though against *one enemy,* are so much higher than those of the last, where *all India* and the great powers of Europe *were united* against us, that it can only be maintained by the transmission of treasure from England, and *by laying fresh burthens upon this exhausted country.*

He is impeached for the means he took *to furnish supplies for carrying on the war.*

To those who think Mr. Hastings violated the law, in accepting presents for the

Company's use, or in withdrawing the guarantee from the Begum without full proof of her delinquency; I answer, he had no other means—Lord North was not disposed to send *him* five hundred thousand pounds in specie, nor as many pence, when his Lordship heard of the invasion of the Carnatic by Hyder; nor to encourage him to exert himself by a vote of parliamentary approbation. On the contrary, Mr. Hastings had every possible species of counteraction at home to struggle against. Let me ask those who disapprove of the guarantee of the Begum having been withdrawn; Is the measure as strong, by many degrees, as that lately adopted in India? One of the contracting parties violates a solemn treaty, because it supposes, that the express provision made by that treaty for an *emergency that has occurred*, will not be efficient; or in other words, unless they take the entire management of of the Carnatic and Tanjore, they may fail in their resources for the war.

I have

I have now gone through the great leading points relative to the Government of India—I defy any candid man to consider the subject truly without being struck with astonishment at the monstrous inconsistency of the King's Ministers: the observation cannot in this sense apply to you, I allow.

You have certainly been consistent. You and your friends have maintained that Mr. Hastings has desolated provinces, has overturned ancient establishments, has violated private property; and that therefore it was right to impeach him.

The Ministers have done the reverse of all this; they have said that he has preserved an empire in a season of the utmost danger, difficulty and distress; that he has improved the resources, and that nothing he did in the management of the revenues of Bengal, was worthy reprehension; yet, when you left them in a minority in a Committee of the
whole

whole Houſe, they permitted you to do and ſay what you pleaſed, though in *manifeſt*, *direct*, and *poſitive contradiction* to *their own Budget*. Your friends have ſaid, that it was in the higheſt degree criminal to demand under any circumſtances a rupee beyond his annual rent from Cheyt Sing, a Zemindar of the Company, and have therefore very correctly argued, that for every ſubſequent meaſure taken in ſupport of a demand originally unjuſt, Mr. Haſtings is fully reſponſible.

The Miniſter defended and proved the juſtice of the demand, and the criminality of the man who delayed to comply with it, but he conceived an *intended puniſhment* never communicated, to exceed an *actual offence*. Yet he very calmly and without farther heſitation allowed your friends to preſent their accuſation as they choſe to draw it out, though in direct oppoſition to the Miniſter's avowed ſentiments.

In

In a word, the Impeachment of Mr. Haftings taken in this point of view, muft ftrike you in the manner it does every rational man, as the moft monftrous abfurdity that ever difgraced a civilized country.

But it was undertaken to retrieve the character of Great Britain in India, fay the friends of Mr. Pitt—How, or in what way? Has any inclination been fhewn by any one man connected with Minifters, to give up one fingle advantage that Mr. Haftings procured for the nation? Does any one think of placing in the Zenana of the Begum, the fixty lacks of rupees that were taken from her eunuchs? or of giving the Nabob Vifier credit for the ten lacks of rupees which were prefented by him to Mr. Haftings, and by Mr. Haftings to the Company? Is there an idea of reftoring Cheyt Sing? On the contrary, has not Mr. Pitt put his name to a letter to Bengal, in which it is
faid,

said, that no idea of his restoration *ever was entertained?* Does not Mr. Dundas plume himself, year after year, upon the flourishing state of the revenue? Has he ever encouraged your idea of reducing the Jumma? Is he not obliged to approve, in the hour of present distress, of a most unequivocal breach of treaty?

Let any one Gentleman read the curious resolutions moved by Mr. Dundas in 1782, that code of laws for India, and then let him consider what attention has been paid to the principles there laid down—With a surplus revenue of more than two millions sterling in Bengal, would you not suppose, that the Minister who avowed it to be a breach of treaty to withhold the payment of the Mogul's tribute, would order it to be punctually discharged hereafter, the moment the purse of Bengal was open to him?

Mr.

Mr. Fox undoubtedly proceeded upon a very different plan. His bills profeſſed to remedy all that Mr. Burke ſtated to be oppreſſion in India, and all that his articles have ſince deſcribed as acts of oppreſſion. Under his clauſes he muſt have aboliſhed the monopolies of ſalt and opium; he muſt have reſtored Cheyt Sing; he muſt have paid to the Mogul his arrears of tribute, and continued an annual payment of twenty-ſix lacks to the preſent hour. Many millions ſterling would have been required to carry the proviſions of his bill into effect.

Fiat juſtitia ruat cœlum.

But Parliament by its annual votes has in effect ſtamped the meaſures of Mr. Haſtings with their fulleſt approbation, while it permits him to remain impeached through life, for adopting them; a truth your friends are fully as ſenſible of as I am, though in this

this moment of compromise they will not so readily acknowledge it.

I have made this letter much longer than I originally intended, but before I conclude it, allow me to mention a very curious circumstance, which I only discovered yesterday.

The Impeachment of Mr. Hastings turned a good deal upon Mr. Sheridan's famous speech in the Begum charge; it received your warmest and most active support.

As far as I had seen upon the records, you had upon all occasions taken the part of the Nabob *against the Begum,* when in Bengal; and, in particular, you declared she ought not to be permitted to leave the dominions, and to carry with her the *immense treasures said to be in her possession,* without her sovereign's consent, although those treasures were at that time *guaranteed* to her by the Company.

In July, 1779, Sir Eyre Coote propofed, that the donation granted to the army by the late Sujah Dowlah, in 1774, fhould be demanded from the prefent Nabob. The Board difcuffed this fubject on the 9th of Auguft, 1779. You contended, *that the Begum ought to pay this money, becaufe all the treafures of Sujah Dowlah came into her poffeffion; that this was a fair demand upon thofe treafures, being promifed by Sujah Dowlah in his life-time*; and even if he had bequeathed the Begum all his treafures, they muft by every law have been charged with the debts he owed: to this Mr. Barwell objected, becaufe we had guaranteed to the Begum all the treafures which might be in her poffeffion on the 16th of November, 1775, in confequence of what fhe then gave up (fifty lacks.) To this you make the following reply,

reply, which is so great a curiosity, considering the part you have acted, that I shall give it at length, not invidiously, I assure you, but in the humble hope, that on better consideration you will feel concern for the violences into which you have been led by others:

Mr. FRANCIS.—" I beg it may be un-
" derstood that I do not acquiesce in any
" part of the preceding Minutes, *that re-*
" *spect the circumstances of the Begum and*
" *her son*, though it would lead me too far
" to enter into a refutation of it at this time.
" On one fact I beg leave only to observe,
" that the Agreement, alluded to by Mr.
" Barwell, was for thirty lacks only, *of*
" *which I am almost certain from memory,*
" *that no more than two-thirds were paid*;
" but be this as it may, the donation mo-
" ney, as I understand it, is due, not from
" the present Nabob, *but from the person*
" *who*

"who inherited or got possession of the personal property of the late Vifier; consequently the demand, if made on the Begum, is not on account of the present Nabob; *nor would it be any violation of the Agreement above-mentioned, supposing that Agreement to have been faithfully executed on her part.*"

If this doctrine be true, what becomes of your charge? For it must apply, and so it ought, *to all the money Sujah Dowlah owed when he died.* The present Nabob succeeded to an empty treasury; but he was indebted sixty lacks to the Company, and to his army double that sum. His troops were in general nine months in arrears when Sujah Dowlah died: so that, in fact, admitting the Begum has become possessed of the treasures by gift or by will, which you know was not the case, she should have given up one hundred and ninety lacks of rupees;

rupees; whereas, suppofing her to have paid the full fum of twenty-fix lacks, and thirty lacks in 1775, which I believe, with you, fhe never did pay, and that the fixty lacks taken from her eunuchs in 1782 are added, there is ftill a very confiderable balance, upon your mode of reckoning, due from her to her fon.

With this anecdote, which is of a fingular kind indeed, I fhall clofe my letter, affuring you, however you may look upon any thing which comes from me, as coming from Mr. Haftings, that he has never feen a line of this letter, nor, indeed, have I feen him fince I began to write it. I did conceive it to be a juftice due from me to Mr. Lufhington, to prove by *authentic documents*, that he was fully juftified in afferting what he did in the Houfe; and I did think that from a fair and candid review of paft and prefent tranfactions

tions in India, you and I might agree in lamenting the inconsistency of our countrymen.

I have the honour to be,

SIR,

Your most obedient,

Humble servant,

JOHN SCOTT.

THE END.

NEW PUBLICATIONS

Printed for J. DEBRETT.

MAJOR SCOTT's SPEECH on Mr. BURKE's MOTION for clofing the Profecution againft Mr. HASTINGS with the Article of Contracts; with a Preface and Notes.

The Preface contains an Account of the late CONTESTS between the Government of FORT ST. GEORGE and the NABOB of ARCOT; the Notes and Copies of the official Documents figned by Mr. DUNDAS, in approbation of various acts which form part of the Articles of Impeachment voted in the laft Parliament.

"Infamy muft necefsarily fall fomewhere."
Mr. BURKE's Speech, Feb. 14, 1779.

OBSERVATIONS on Mr. DUNDAS's INDIA BUDGET of 1790. Price 1s. 6d.

A MAP of CRANGANORE and JAYCOTTAH, with the adjacent Countries; fhewing their exact Situations and Connection with the Dominions of TIPPOO SULTAUN and the RAJAH of TRAVANCORE.——Drawn on the Spot.

The EAST INDIA KALENDAR; or, ASIATIC REGISTER: for
BENGAL,
MADRAS,
BOMBAY,
FORT MARLBOROUGH,
CHINA, and
ST. HELENA,
FOR THE YEAR 1791.

On a more extenfive PLAN than any hitherto offered to the Public. Containing complete and correct Lifts of the Civil, Military, Marine, Law, and Revenue Eftablifhments, Public Offices, Bankers; Greek, Armenian, Mogul, and Portuguefe Merchants; Company's Agents at Home and Abroad; with a correct Lift of Britifh European Subjects refiding in India, not in the Company's fervice, &c. &c.

A NEW EDITION, carefully corrected to the PRESENT TIME, including the late PROMOTIONS both at HOME and in INDIA.—To be continued annually, Price 2s. 6d. fewed.

A SHORT REVIEW of the TRADE of the EAST INDIA COMPANY, between the YEARS 1785 and 1790. Taken from Papers before the HOUSE OF COMMONS. Price 2s.

An INQUIRY into the SITUATION of the EAST INDIA COMPANY, from Papers laid before the Houfe of Commons, in 1787, 1788, 1789, and 1790, with an Appendix of interefting Papers. By George Craufurd, Efq. Price 6s.

The REAL SITUATION of the EAST INDIA COMPANY confidered, with refpect to their Rights and Privileges, under the Operation of the late Acts of Parliament. By George Tierney, Efq. With an Appendix of Original Papers. Price 2s. 6d.

An EXPLANATION of the MISTAKEN PRINCIPLE on which the COMMUTATION was FOUNDED. By Thomas Bates Rous, Efq. Price 1s. 6d.

Publications Printed for J. Debrett.

JOURNAL of a VOYAGE to PORT JACKSON, in NEW SOUTH WALES, with a full and accurate Account of his Majesty's Settlement there, a Description of the Natives, and of the Natural Productions of New Holland; a correct Diary of the Weather, Latitudes, Longitudes, &c. &c.——By JOHN WHITE, Esq. Surgeon-General to the Settlement, and Corresponding Member of the Medical Society in London.

Illustrated with Sixty-five elegant Engravings, from Drawings copied from Nature by Miss STONE, Mr. NODDER, Mr. CATTON, &c. and exhibiting near One Hundred Figures of non-descript Birds, Lizards, curious Cones of Trees, Animals, &c. of New South Wales, accompanied with scientific Descriptions, and an elegant engraved Title Page and Vignette, by MILTON.——In One Volume, Royal 4to. price 1l. 16s. in boards; or with Sixty-five Plates, beautifully coloured after the Originals, price 3l. 6s. in boards.

JOURNAL of a VOYAGE from PORT JACKSON, New SOUTH WALES, to CANTON, in 1788, through an unexplored Passage. By Thomas Gilbert, Esq. Commander of the Charlotte. Illustrated with Views of the following Islands discovered on the Passage, viz. Chatham's, Ibbitson's, Matthews, Calvert's, Knox's, Daniel's, Marlar's, and Gilbert's. Elegantly printed in Quarto. Price 8s. sewed.

The PARLIAMENTARY REGISTER of the PRESENT SESSION; No. III. and IV. Price 2s. Containing the Three Debates on the Important Question, "Whether an IMPEACHMENT abated by the Dissolution of Parliament?"

To which is added, A List of the Proceedings touching the Question of the Continuance of Impeachments, and other Parliamentary Proceedings from Parliament to Parliament.

The PARLIAMENTARY REGISTER, from 1780 to 1784, in 14 Volumes. Price 5l. 5s. half-bound and lettered.

The PARLIAMENTARY REGISTER, from 1784 to 1790, in 13 Volumes. Price 6l. 12s. half-bound and lettered.

A SKETCH of the REIGN of GEORGE the THIRD, from 1780 to the Close of the Year 1790; the fourth Edition, Price 4s.

A VINDICATION of Mr. BURKE's REFLECTIONS on the Revolution in France, in Answer to all his Opponents. Price 2s. 6d.

A LETTER to the Right Honorable EDMUND BURKE, from Sir BROOKE BOOTHBY, Bart. The Second Edition, with Additions. Price 2s. 6d.

THOUGHTS on GOVERNMENT, occasioned by Mr. Burke's Reflections. The fourth Edition. To which is added, A Postscript, in Reply to a Vindication of Mr. Burke. By George Rous, Esq. Price 2s.

The SUBSTANCE of the Speech of the MARQUIS of LANSDOWN, Dec. 14, 1790, on the Convention with Spain. Price 1s.

An ANSWER to Mr. BURKE's REFLECTIONS. By M. De Pont. Price 1s.

www.ingramcontent.com/pod-product-compliance
Lightning Source LLC
Chambersburg PA
CBHW020140170426
43199CB00010B/826